Meet My Mouse

Written by Fay Robinson   **Photographs by Dwight R. Kuhn**

ScottForesman

A Division of HarperCollinsPublishers

My mouse has round, black eyes.
Like all mice, she has oval ears
and a pointed nose.

My mouse has brown and white spots
Like all mice, she has very soft fur.

My mouse has long whiskers.
Like all mice, she uses her whiskers
to feel things around her.

My mouse has long teeth.
Like all mice, her teeth keep
growing. She chews things to keep
her teeth from growing too long.

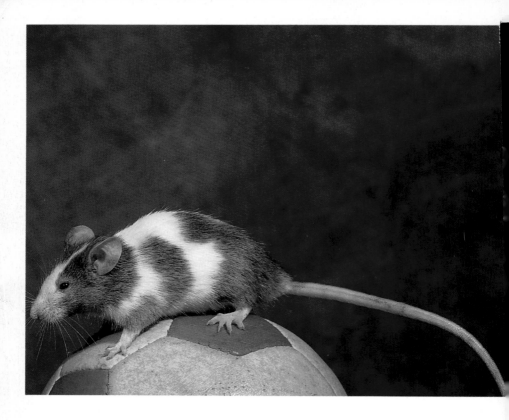

My mouse has a long, thin tail.
Like all mice, her tail is as long
as her body.

10

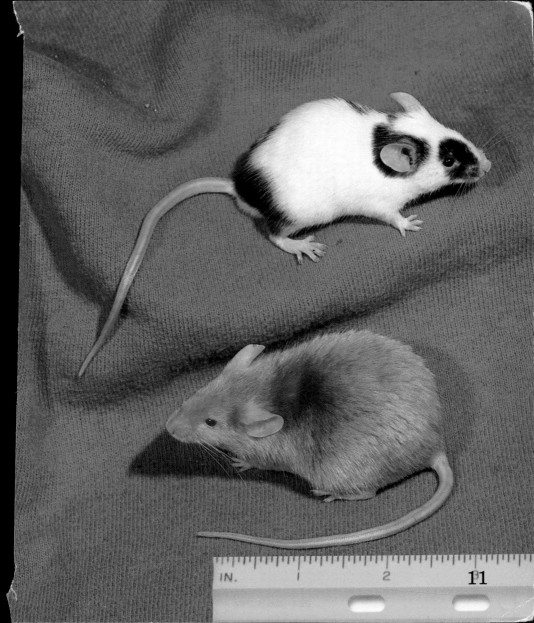

My mouse has lots to do.
Like all mice, she runs, climbs,
jumps, digs, and eats.

My mouse is a great pet.
Would you like a pet mouse?

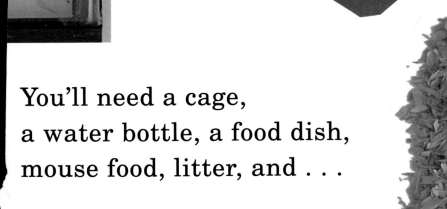

You'll need a cage,
a water bottle, a food dish,
mouse food, litter, and . . .

your own mouse!